RESCUING Animals FROM DISASTERS
SAVING ANIMALS FROM
FIRES

by Stephen Person

Consultants: John Griffin
Director, Humane Wildlife Services

Trish Jackman
Project Wildlife
Wildlife Rehabilitation Manager

Shawnie Williams
Skyhunters Raptor Rehabilitation and Education Center
Wildlife Specialist

BEARPORT
PUBLISHING

New York, New York

Credits

Cover and Title Page, © Chris Butler/Idaho Statesman/MCT/Landov; 4, © San Diego Union Tribune/John Gastaldo/Zuma Press; 5, © San Diego Union Tribune/John Gibbins/Zuma Press; 6, © UPI/Earl S. Cryer/Landov; 7, © San Diego Union Tribune/John Gastaldo/Zuma Press; 8, © AP Photo/Reed Saxon; 10L, © US Forest Service/Time & Life Pictures/Getty Images; 10R, Courtesy of Smithsonian Institution Archives; 11L, © K.J. Historical/Corbis; 11R, © Imagebroker/SuperStock; 12L, © Eric Thayer/Getty Images; 12R, © Mario Anzuoni/Reuters/Landov; 13T, © Dan Dadmun; 13B, © Zuma Press/Newscom; 14L, © Ray Eubanks/The HSUS; 14R, © Christine Jensen/The HSUS; 15T, © The HSUS; 15B, © Christine Jensen/The HSUS; 16, © Andreas Hartl; 17T, © Tonto National Forest/Todd Willard; 17B, © Tonto National Forest/Todd Willard; 18, © Minden Pictures/SuperStock; 19T, © Robert Cianflone/Getty Images; 19B, Courtesy of Wildlife Victoria; 20, © Minden Pictures/SuperStock; 21T, © Reuters/Courtesy of the Department of Sustainability and Environment/Mark Pardew/Landov; 21B, © AP Photo; 22, © AP Photo/Keith D. Cullom; 23, © Zuma Press/Newscom; 24, Courtesy photo by the Boulder Camera; 25, © Helen H. Richardson/The Denver Post; 26, © Helen H. Richardson/The Denver Post; 27, © Helen H. Richardson/The Denver Post; 28, © David Chapman/RSPCA Photolibrary; 29, © Michael Booth/IFAW/AFP/Getty Images/Newscom; 31, © Tom Grundy/Shutterstock.

Publisher: Kenn Goin
Editorial Director: Adam Siegel
Creative Director: Spencer Brinker
Design: Dawn Beard Creative and Kim Jones
Photo Researcher: Picture Perfect Professionals, LLC

Library of Congress Cataloging-in-Publication Data

Person, Stephen.
    Saving animals from fires / by Stephen Person.
        p. cm. — (Rescuing animals from disasters)
    Includes bibliographical references and index.
    ISBN-13: 978-1-61772-293-6 (library binding)
    ISBN-10: 1-61772-293-6 (library binding)
    1. Animal rescue—Juvenile literature. 2. Fires—Juvenile literature. I. Title.
    QL83.2.P477 2012
    636.08'32—dc22

                                                    2011010199

For more information, write to Bearport Publishing Company, Inc., 45 West 21st Street, Suite 3B, New York, New York 10010. Printed in the United States of America in North Mankato, Minnesota.

071511
042711CGD

10 9 8 7 6 5 4 3 2 1

CONTENTS

Mountains on Fire

It was 3:00 in the morning on October 27, 2003—but Nancy Baar did not dare go to sleep. She looked up at the mountains rising east of her home near San Diego, California. A huge **wildfire** lit up the night. Bright orange flames danced and leaped down the slopes, moving closer and closer to her home.

On October 27, 2003, people in San Diego looked up to see the mountains on fire.

Suddenly, a police car skidded to a stop in front of her house. An officer told her that she had ten minutes to pack everything up and go. Nancy had to leave quickly, but it wouldn't be easy. Her **property** was home to dogs, a horse, a pig, and 71 birds! How could she move all those animals to safety?

This picture shows the Cedar Fire nearing homes in San Diego, California.

The huge wildfire burning near Nancy's home became known as the Cedar Fire. It began on October 25 and burned until November 4. One of the deadliest wildfires in the history of California, it destroyed about 2,800 buildings.

A Late-Night Rescue

Nancy rushed to save the animals around her home. Luckily, she had already loaded her dogs and horse into a van when she saw the flames getting close to her house. A police officer lifted her pig into the back of his patrol car. Yet Nancy still needed to save her birds. She had time to grab about 30 of them—but was forced to leave more than 40 others behind. The birds were not forgotten, though.

Horses near the Cedar Fire were loaded into horse trailers and carried to a safe location.

The police officer made a phone call to Darrell Hanson, who worked at a nearby **animal shelter**. Darrell leaped out of bed and raced over in his truck to Nancy's property. He ran from cage to cage, putting birds into empty dog and cat carrying crates. "They squawked and put up a fuss," he said, but there was little time to waste. With giant flames raging less than a quarter of a mile (.4 km) away, Darrell and the birds barely escaped the spreading fire. He brought the rescued birds to people who would keep them until they could be **reunited** with Nancy.

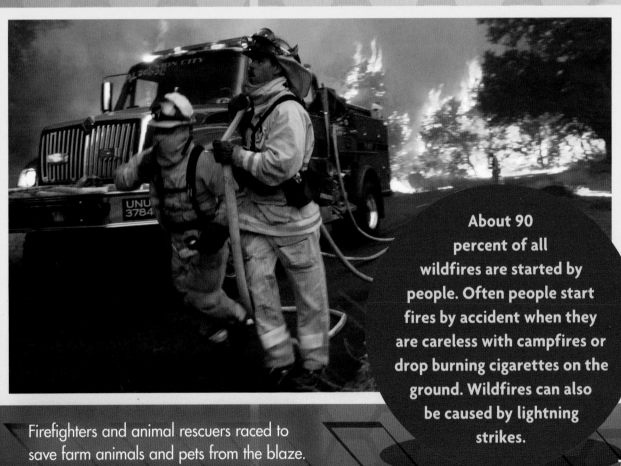

Firefighters and animal rescuers raced to save farm animals and pets from the blaze.

About 90 percent of all wildfires are started by people. Often people start fires by accident when they are careless with campfires or drop burning cigarettes on the ground. Wildfires can also be caused by lightning strikes.

When Fire Is Wild

How had the fire that threatened to kill Nancy, her pets, and thousands of other people and animals gotten so big? One reason is that Southern California had been going through a long **drought**. Years of hot, dry weather had caused grasses, bushes, and trees to dry out. When wood and grass are dry, they burn more quickly.

When winds are blowing, wildfires can spread quickly—moving at a speed of 16 miles per hour (26 kph), and sometimes even greater.

To make things worse, strong winds were blowing when the Cedar Fire began. Winds can quickly spread fire by blowing flames from tree to tree. All that was needed to start a wildfire was a source of heat to **ignite** the flames. It came from a hunter who got lost in Cleveland National Forest, 25 miles (40 km) east of San Diego. On October 25, he lit a small fire, hoping it would help rescuers find him. Unfortunately, the fire spread into nearby bushes—and the massive Cedar Fire began.

The Cedar Fire

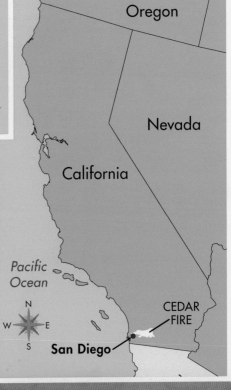

After a few days, the Cedar Fire eventually started moving toward a part of the forest that had been destroyed by an earlier fire in 2002. When the flames reached this area, the lack of wood caused the fire to stop spreading.

The Cedar Fire burned more than 280,000 acres (113,312 hectares).

Smokey Bear

When wildfires spread through forests, they can be very dangerous to the animals that live there. In 1950, a huge wildfire ripped through Lincoln National Forest in New Mexico. While battling the blaze, firefighters spotted a black bear **cub** clinging to a branch high in a tree. The tiny bear's paws and legs were badly burned. Unable to find the cub's mother, the firefighters took the bear to a **veterinarian** in Santa Fe.

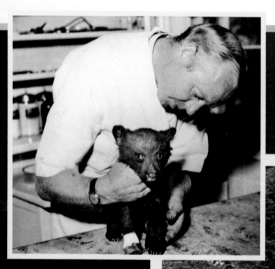

A veterinarian examines the paws of Smokey after he was rescued. The little bear weighed just five pounds (2.3 kg).

Smokey as an adult at the National Zoo

After Smokey was rescued, he was moved to the National Zoo in Washington, D.C. The famous cub got so much fan mail that the U.S. Postal Service gave him his own zip code!

Rescuers soon began calling the cub Smokey. As the baby bear recovered, his story was told in newspapers all over the country. As a result, it didn't take long for Smokey to become a **symbol** of the dangers of wildfires. The U.S. Forest Service used his story to teach people about how wildfires harm animals—and what people can do to help **prevent** starting the deadly blazes.

Smokey posters and advertisements are still used to teach people not to be careless with fire in the woods.

PLEASE!

SMOKEY

Only you can prevent forest fires

FIRE DANGER

HIGH

TODAY!

PREVENT FOREST FIRES

Signs like this one warn visitors when forests are hot and dry, making wildfires more likely.

Rescue Lessons

In the years since Smokey's rescue, people have learned a lot about saving animals from fires. For example, many pet owners now know that they have to be prepared to move quickly in case of a fire. They should have crates ready so they can take their pets with them when they **evacuate** their homes.

During the San Diego wildfires of 2007, people brought their pets with them to evacuation centers like this county fairground.

If people are forced to leave their homes without their pets or farm animals, they should leave a list behind for firefighters. The list should describe each animal and tell where it can be found. Firefighters and animal rescuers can use this list to find the animals quickly and get them to safety.

Big farm animals, such as horses and cows, however, can't be driven off in a car. How do they stay safe during a fire? Luckily, some people have devoted their lives to rescuing them. In 2007, major wildfires spread across Southern California. Daniel Desousa of San Diego's Department of Animal Services was ready. Racing from farm to farm, Daniel loaded animals into vans. "We're doing the best we can to keep ahead of the flames and pull the animals out," Daniel said. He and other rescuers saved thousands of horses.

During the 2007 fires in Southern California, horses and llamas were brought to evacuation areas all over San Diego. Some even lived in parking lots until it was safe to return home.

Burned by the Flames

Pets and farm animals have owners to rescue them—but what about wild animals? They know that fire is dangerous. Their **instincts** tell them to run or fly from the flames. However, if they are unable to move fast enough, they can be trapped and burned. The good news is that there are people who are willing to care for these wild animals.

Chuck and Cindy Traisi ran The Fund for Animals Wildlife Center for 25 years. During that time, they helped more than 15,000 injured animals, including cougars, a hippopotamus, and this African lion, named Samson.

During the 2007 San Diego wildfires, rescuers searched the woods for **victims**. Injured animals were brought to The Fund for Animals Wildlife Center in Southern California for medical care. One victim was a young gray fox with burned feet and fur. Workers at the center cleaned and bandaged the fox's injuries and gave him medicine. When the gray fox had healed, he was released back into the wild.

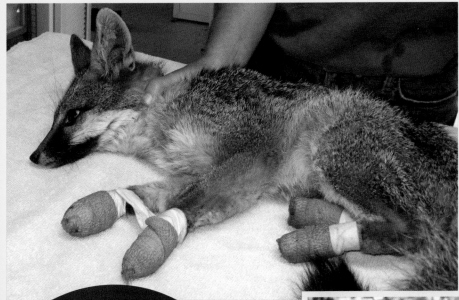

After his burns healed, the gray fox seemed very excited to be set free.

The 2007 San Diego wildfires got so close to the wildlife center, workers had to evacuate. Chuck Traisi risked his life to stay behind with the animals that could not be easily moved. Luckily, the fire never reached the wildlife center.

Danger Underwater

Since fish live in the water, it may seem like they would be safe from wildfires—but this is not always true. In June 2005, the massive Cave Creek Complex fire raged in central Arizona. **Biologists** realized the burning trees were creating clouds of **ash**. If the ash fell into nearby creeks, it would **pollute** the water. As a result, fish would not be able to get the **oxygen** they need to breathe and would die from **suffocation**. Biologist Chris Cantrell was worried about the Gila topminnow, an **endangered species** of fish that lives in Lime Creek—which was very close to the flames.

The Gila topminnow grows to be just two inches (5 cm) long.

To save the rare fish, Chris joined a team that hiked four miles (6.4 km) to Lime Creek. Using nets, the scientists pulled out about 200 Gila topminnows. The scientists kept the rescued fish in tanks. Over time, rain cleared the ash from Lime Creek, and the fish were returned to their natural **habitat**.

A team of biologists went in search of Gila topminnows. "We realized they were in trouble and wanted to do something right away," said Chris Cantrell.

Scientists used nets to pull the endangered fish out of Lime Creek.

The Gila topminnow lives in a small number of creeks and rivers in Arizona and Mexico. If the Gila topminnows in Lime Creek had been killed, the species would have been closer to **extinction**.

Disaster in Australia

In February 2009, huge wildfires began spreading through the forests of southeast Australia. One kind of animal, called a **wombat**, was able to hide safely underground in its **burrows**. However, once the wombats left their tunnel-like homes, they discovered that the fires had destroyed their forest—leaving them with nothing to eat.

Wombats eat grasses, bark, and roots. This food supply was destroyed by the wildfires, leaving wombats in danger of starving.

Drought, strong winds, and temperatures of more than 115°F (46°C) led to the massive wildfires of 2009. These fires were the deadliest in Australian history, killing more than 200 people. Scientists fear that millions of animals might have died in the blaze.

Other animals, such as kangaroos, were able to outrun the flames—but they were not safe for long. Some returned home while the ground was still hot and burned their feet.

Starving wombats, burned kangaroos, and many more wild animals needed help. Luckily for them, animal rescuers hiked into the still-smoking forests. They took the injured animals to shelters, where they were given food and medical care. Once the animals were healthy again, they were released into unburned areas of the forest where they could safely live.

These baby kangaroos, called joeys, lost their parents in the wildfires. They would not have survived without the help of animal rescuers.

A kangaroo recovering from its burns

Sam the Koala

While kangaroos can move quickly and wombats can hide in their burrows, koalas have a harder time escaping wildfires. These furry animals spend most of their time in trees—which quickly get burned during a blaze. On the ground the animals move slowly, so it's hard for them to get away from speeding flames.

People often call koalas "koala bears"—but they are not bears at all. Koalas are **marsupials**, a group of animals that raise and carry their babies in pouches on their stomachs. Kangaroos and wombats are also marsupials.

When a **volunteer** firefighter named David Tree was searching for injured animals during the 2009 Australia wildfires, he came across a koala with badly burned paws. "You all right, buddy?" David asked. As he slowly stepped closer, he held out a cold bottle of water and helped the injured koala take a drink. Pictures of this event soon appeared in newspapers and on the Internet. The koala, nicknamed Sam, became famous. After rescuing her, David took the koala to a wildlife shelter, where she was treated for her burns.

This picture was seen all over the world, making Sam famous.

Sam recovering from her burns at the wildlife shelter

Unlikely Friends

In the race to save animals from fires, surprising things can happen. In May 2009, a wildfire burned in a forest near Santa Barbara, California. Wildlife rescuer Julia Di Sieno rushed in to help. First Julia helped rescue a three-week-old bobcat from the flames. Then she found a three-day-old deer. They were both brought back to the rescue team's office.

Severe droughts in California helped wildfires like this one in Santa Barbara spread quickly.

Wildfires can happen all over the United States, but they are most common in the West. This is because the West has many large forests, and summers in western states are usually hot and dry.

With no empty crates left that were large enough to hold the **fawn**, Julia took a huge risk. She placed the fawn in the same room with the bobcat kitten—even though adult bobcats often attack and eat young deer. Surprisingly, when the bobcat saw the fawn, it ran up to the young deer and curled up with its new friend!

The bobcat kitten and fawn cuddled up together on the floor of the animal rescue team's office.

The Holiday Fire Mystery

The timing of a wildfire can sometimes put animals at risk. On September 6, 2010, a wildfire began spreading in a forest near Boulder, Colorado. It was Labor Day, and many families were away from home for the holiday. All over Boulder, pets were home alone—and in danger.

Ranch workers near Boulder worked quickly to evacuate horses from ranches near the wildfire.

Terrified pet owners called Boulder government **officials** and gave them addresses where their pets could be found. A group of rescuers called Red Star Animal Emergency Services drove to the houses and removed dogs, cats, birds, and other pets. The animals were taken to shelters, and owners came to pick them up. Only one pet was not claimed, a badly burned black cat that had been found hiding outside under a rock. Veterinarians named him Sizzle. Although the cat's burns slowly began to heal, no one knew who his owner was. Would the two ever be reunited?

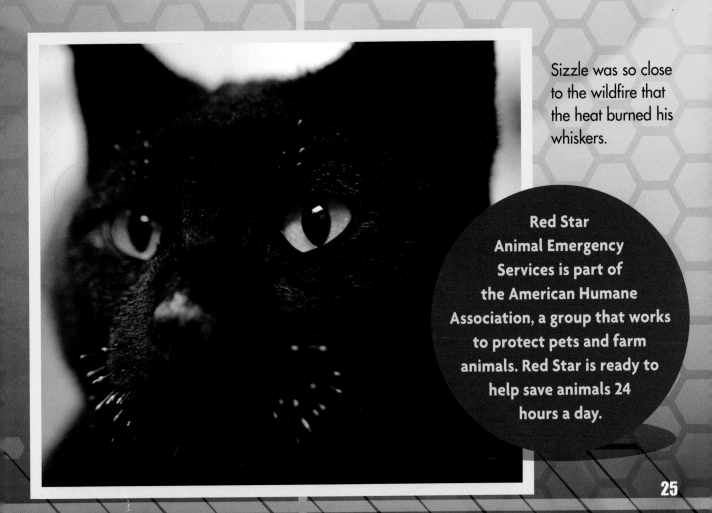

Sizzle was so close to the wildfire that the heat burned his whiskers.

Red Star Animal Emergency Services is part of the American Humane Association, a group that works to protect pets and farm animals. Red Star is ready to help save animals 24 hours a day.

Sizzle's Happy Ending

About two weeks after Sizzle had been rescued from the fire, a woman named Lori Church picked up a newspaper in Denver, about 25 miles (40 km) from Boulder. She read a story about Sizzle and was shocked by how much the cat sounded like her cat, Morgan. Lori's cat had been missing for about a month. Could he have wandered all the way to Boulder? Could Sizzle really be Morgan?

Veterinarians treated Sizzle for burns on all four legs and paws.

Lori called the animal hospital in Boulder. She described Morgan to the vet who had been taking care of Sizzle. It sounded like Sizzle might indeed be her cat. Full of hope, Lori drove to Boulder. When she was there, she told the vet that her cat had a long scar on his front right leg. The vet gently unwrapped the bandages from Sizzle's leg—and there was the scar. At last, two friends who had never expected to see each other again were reunited!

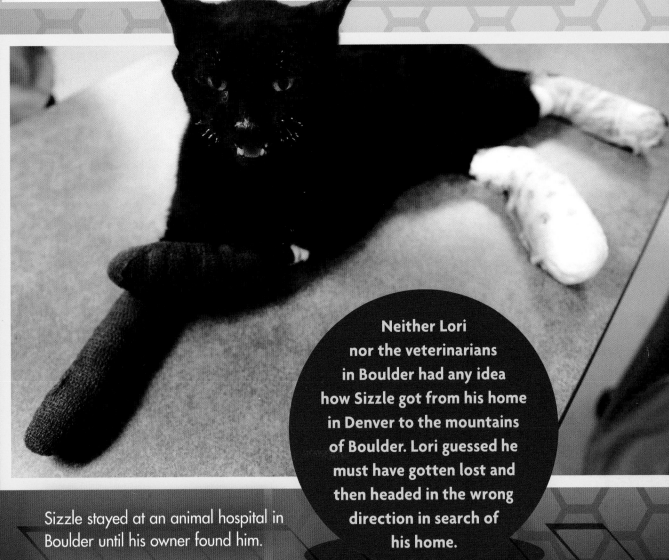

Sizzle stayed at an animal hospital in Boulder until his owner found him.

Neither Lori nor the veterinarians in Boulder had any idea how Sizzle got from his home in Denver to the mountains of Boulder. Lori guessed he must have gotten lost and then headed in the wrong direction in search of his home.

FAMOUS WILDFIRES AND RESCUES

In recent years, long droughts and hot weather have led to huge wildfires in many parts of the world. Here are two major fires that put animals in danger.

Russian Wildfires, Russia, 2010

- In parts of Russia, the summer of 2010 was the hottest in more than 100 years. Many forests caught fire and hundreds of wildfires burned at once.

- In early August, a wildfire spread toward an animal shelter near the capital city of Moscow. The shelter is home to dogs and cats, as well as monkeys and bears that were once used as circus animals. Flames got within about 450 feet (137 m) of the shelter before volunteers were able to put out the fire.

A bat roosting in a tree

- The wildfires burned more than two million acres (809,371 hectares) of forest. Scientists are now worried about several animal species, including bats, that used to live there. Bats **roost** in hollow trees, but many of these roosting spots were burned by the wildfires. As a result, the bats have fewer places where they can safely sleep and rest.

Station Fire, Los Angeles, California, 2009

- This huge wildfire began in Angeles National Forest, north of Los Angeles, and quickly spread to more than 100,000 acres (40,469 hectares).

- While thousands of people evacuated with their pets, volunteers raced to gather horses, cows, goats, llamas, pigs, chickens, and other farm animals. The animals were taken to shelters that were out of danger from the fire.

- The fire also threatened the Wildlife Waystation, an animal shelter that is home to hundreds of wild animals, including chimpanzees, lions, tigers, jaguars, and bears. Workers packed the big animals in cages and drove them to safe places such as the Los Angeles Zoo.

ANIMALS AT RISK FROM FIRES

Fires put pets, farm animals, and wild animals at risk. No matter where an animal lives, it may need to be rescued from a fire. Only someone who is specially trained to rescue animals from fires, however, should attempt to save them.

Orangutans

- In the fall of 2006, wildfires in the Southeast Asian country of Indonesia threatened thousands of endangered orangutans living in forests.

- Some orangutans were burned to death by the fire. Others breathed in hot smoke, which can damage their **lungs** and cause death.

- Rescue teams raced into the forests to help. When they spotted an orangutan, rescuers shot the animal with a **tranquilizer gun**. This put the orangutan to sleep so it could be safely carried out of the burning forest. The animals were later released into areas of the forest that were far from the flames.

A rescuer carries a young orangutan to safety. Fewer than 60,000 orangutans live in the forests of Indonesia. That number is falling quickly due to loss of habitat.

Pet Store Animals

- Fires don't have to be wild to put animals in danger. In November 2009, a pet store in Roanoke, Virginia, caught fire.

- Animals in the store were in danger of burning to death or choking from the smoke.

- Pet store workers refused to leave the animals behind in the burning store. Working quickly, they carried dogs, cats, guinea pigs, and other animals outside. No animals were hurt in the fire.

GLOSSARY

animal shelter (AN-uh-muhl SHEL-tur) a place where homeless or injured animals are cared for until they are reunited with their human families or placed in new homes

ash (ASH) a powdery substance that is left after something has burned

biologists (bye-OL-uh-jists) scientists who study animals or plants

burrows (BUR-ohz) holes or tunnels in the ground made or used by an animal as a den or place to live in

cub (KUHB) baby bear

drought (DROUT) a long period with little or no rain

endangered species (en-DAYN-jurd SPEE-sheez) a kind of animal that is in danger of dying out completely

evacuate (i-VAK-yoo-*ayt*) to move away from an area that is dangerous

extinction (ek-STINGK-shuhn) when a type of animal or plant dies out completely

fawn (FAWN) a young deer

habitat (HAB-uh-*tat*) the place in nature where a plant or animal normally lives

ignite (ig-NITE) to set on fire or catch fire

instincts (IN-stingkts) knowledge and ways of acting that an animal is born with and that help it survive

lungs (LUHNGZ) parts of the body in a person's or an animal's chest that are used for breathing

marsupials (mar-SOO-pee-uhlz) a group of mammals in which the young are raised in pouches found on the mothers' bellies

officials (uh-FISH-uhlz) people who hold offices or important positions

oxygen (OK-suh-juhn) a colorless gas that is found in the air and water, and that animals and people need to breathe

pollute (puh-LOOT) to damage the air, water, or land with harmful materials

prevent (pri-VENT) to stop something from happening

property (PROP-ur-tee) a piece of land

reunited (*ree*-yoo-NITE-id) joined or brought together again

roost (ROOST) to rest or sleep in a particular place

suffocation (*suhf*-uh-KAY-shuhn) being killed by having one's supply of air stopped

symbol (SIM-buhl) something that stands for something else

tranquilizer gun (TRANG-kwuh-*lye*-zur GUN) a gun that shoots a drug into animals to calm them or make them fall asleep

veterinarian (*vet*-ur-uh-NER-ee-uhn) a doctor who cares for animals

victims (VIK-tuhmz) people or animals who are hurt, injured, or killed by something or someone

volunteer (*vol*-uhn-TIHR) a person who does a job without pay to help others

wildfire (WILDE-*fire*) a fire that spreads quickly over a large area, usually in the wilderness

wombat (WOM-bat) an animal that lives in Australia and looks like a small bear

BIBLIOGRAPHY

The Fund for Animals (www.fundforanimals.org/)

The San Diego Wildfires Education Project (http://interwork.sdsu.edu/fire/purpose.htm)

U.S. Fish & Wildlife Service: Fire Management (www.fws.gov/fire/)

READ MORE

Betancourt, Jeanne. *Ten True Animal Rescues.* New York: Scholastic (1998).

Costain, Meredith. *Devouring Flames: The Story of Forest Fires.* Washington, D.C.: National Geographic Society (2006).

Houser, Sue. *Hot Foot Teddy: The True Story of Smokey Bear.* Evansville, IN: M.T. Publishing Company (2006).

Trammel, Howard K. *Wildfires (A True Book).* New York: Children's Press (2009).

LEARN MORE ONLINE

To learn more about rescuing animals from fires, visit
www.bearportpublishing.com/RescuingAnimalsfromDisasters

INDEX

ABOUT THE AUTHOR

Stephen Person has written many children's books about history, science, and the environment. He lives with his family in Saratoga Springs, New York.